Right on the Money

Right on the Money

An introduction to personal
finance from a Christian perspective

Kelvin Worthington

CHRISTIAN
FOCUS

Copyright © Kelvin Worthington 2009

ISBN 978-1-84550-426-7

10 9 8 7 6 5 4 3 2 1

Published in 2009
by
Christian Focus Publications, Geanies House,
Fearn, Ross-shire, IV20 1TW, Scotland.

www.christianfocus.com

Cover design by Paul Lewis

Printed and bound by Norhaven, Denmark

Contents

About the Author 7

Introduction 9

Chapter 1 – Overview 13

Chapter 2 – The Basics 21

Chapter 3 – Budgeting 37

Chapter 4 – Investing 45

Chapter 5 – Retirement Planning 59

Chapter 6 – Protecting Your Family 65

Chapter 7 – Other Matters 73

Appendix – Example of Personal Budget 93

About the Author

Kelvin Worthington has over 25 years' experience in Corporate and Business Banking, both in the UK and Australia. He currently runs his own business, advising clients on the setting up and running of their own business. During his time in the UK he was a Small Business Advisor for a major UK bank and also a volunteer Business Mentor with the Prince's Youth Business Trust, a charitable organisation set up to help young people establish and run their own business.

Kelvin has an Honours Degree in Financial Services from the University of Central England, UK. His degree disciplines include Accounting, Strategic Management, Marketing, Management of Company Finance, Strategic Management of IT, Statistics, Decision Techniques and Quantitative Methods.

Kelvin is also an Associate of the Chartered Institute of

Bankers (London), where he studied subjects including Economics and Investment Strategies.

Married to Helen and currently living in Sydney, Australia, Kelvin is a regular worshipper at Christ Church Lavender Bay. He is also a published author, having written books on subjects such as setting up and running a small business and accountancy.

Introduction

Personal finances can be an area of many people's lives which are not handled well and which may be out of control, causing much stress and hardship to the individuals and their families. It is an area which is easy to get wrong and which can also seem to be very daunting and complex. Christians are not exempt from these issues.

As Christians, we fail to please God if we are less than faithful stewards of all that He has entrusted to us. This includes our dealings with money and finance. As J. C. Ryle puts it, 'Another mark of growth in grace is increased holiness of life and conversation. The man whose soul is growing gets more dominion over sin, the world and the devil every year. He becomes more careful about his temper, his words and his actions. He is more watchful over his conduct in every relation of life' (J. C. Ryle, *Holiness*). If we as Christians are to set an example to the world and be 'salt and light' in this secular society, we need to demonstrate good stewardship and behaviours in all areas of our lives, including the way in which we handle our personal finances. As Jesus says, 'If then you have not been faithful in handling worldly wealth, how can you be trusted with true wealth' (Luke 16:11).

I therefore wanted to write a book about personal finances which would be practical rather than academic – a book which ordinary Christians could read and understand and which would unravel some of the 'mystique' concerning the area of personal finances. At the same time, I wanted to be able to show how the Bible provides us with teaching and guidance on such matters.

The purpose of this book is, therefore, twofold. Firstly, to help Christians (and, for that matter, non-Christians) with their personal finances by providing some general guidance and principles which, if followed, will help them keep their personal finances under control. Secondly, to help Christians understand the special responsibilities being a Christian brings to the area of our personal finances and what Holy Scripture has to say and teach us on such matters. For, as Christians, we have a special responsibility and obligation to live holy lives, and how we handle and deal with our personal finances is a major part of the day-to-day, practical outliving of our faith.

From the Christian perspective this book will deal with issues such as budgeting, debt, retirement planning, investing, tithing, gambling and being responsible with the money which God has entrusted to us. The book will also seek to answer questions which Christians may have, or struggle with from time to time, such as 'Is investing in shares a form of gambling?'; 'Do I need to plan for my retirement or should I just trust God to provide for my needs?'; 'Is it acceptable to buy lottery tickets?'; 'Is it appropriate for me to ensure that my family are protected in the event of my death or should I simply trust that God will take care of them?'; 'Is it wrong of me to have money and material possessions?'; 'If I become a Christian will God bless me with money and material things?' and 'Should I sell everything I have and follow Jesus?'. These are all valid questions which Christians and perhaps non-Christians may ask themselves at some time in their lives, and this book seeks to help answer those questions by applying the teaching of Holy Scripture to the issue concerned.

Lastly, may I say that when my wife suggested I should write this book, I must confess I was unsure as to whether or not to take up the challenge. Whilst I feel well qualified to write about personal finances, having been a bank manager for 25 years and holding recognized qualifications in finance, I am not a biblical scholar and thus feel extremely poorly qualified to interpret what Holy Scripture has to say on these matters. After all, if the apostle Paul can say that he is the 'chief of sinners' (1 Tim. 1:15-16), what does that make me?

However, I have persevered in my task and pray that with God's help and guidance this book will be an accurate reflection of the teaching of Holy Scripture and that also He will bless it to those who read its contents. To Him be all the glory.

Chapter 1 – Overview

It is important to remember that when we become a Christian we are signing up for a lifetime of conflict. Jesus makes it clear that when we become a follower of Him, it brings us into direct conflict with the world and Satan. Satan, whose very nature is deceitful, will use all the tricks in his armoury to trip us up and make us less than effective Christians in this world. He loves it when we backslide or we upset our heavenly Father by saying, doing or thinking something which is inappropriate for a saved Christian. If we doubt that this conflict exists, we need only look at what Jesus says and the terminology used in the Bible. We find that Jesus says, 'I did not come to bring peace but a sword' (Matt. 10:34) and 'Anyone who is not for me is really against me' (Luke 11:23). James continues this theme when he says, 'Don't you know that to be the world's friend is to be God's enemy?' (James 4:4) and John confirms it when he says, 'If you love the world, you do not love the Father' (1 John 2:15). These are clear references to an environment of conflict. We also find elsewhere in the Bible that this picture of a state of conflict is continued when Paul talks of the whole armour of God and says, 'Put on the armour that God gives you, so that you will be able to stand up against Satan's evil tricks. For we are not fighting against human beings but against the wicked spiritual forces in the heavenly world, the rulers, authorities and cosmic powers of this dark age' (Eph. 6:11-12). This is not the language of a serene, peaceful environment, but one where conflict abounds, and we as true Christians are in the thick of it!

Satan will employ many tricks to cause us to be less than effective Christians in this world, and one of these is to cause us to be less than appropriate stewards of the financial resources which God has entrusted to us. When looking at the question of personal finances from a Christian perspective, there are, I feel, a number of key overriding principles which have their roots firmly in Holy Scripture. If we apply these principles at all times then our personal finances will be dealt with in accordance with God's holy law and will be pleasing to Him.

It all belongs to Him

It is important to always be mindful that everything we have comes from God. It is only because of His love for us and through His grace and mercy that we are saved from sin and become true Christians. We cannot earn this, it is a gift from God. As the word 'gift' implies, this is something which is free. It cannot be earned through good deeds, or by giving lots of money to the poor and needy. It is a free gift from a loving heavenly Father who dearly wants us to accept His gift and be saved from sin and eternal death.

In the same way, everything that we have in this world is also a gift from God. In the context of personal finances it is important to always remember that our homes, possessions and money really all belong to God and that we are mere custodians of these gifts while we are here on the earth. Therefore, it is incumbent upon us to use these gifts wisely, as He would want us to, in ways pleasing to Him, and in accordance with the teaching which we find in the Bible. We should not be wasteful with these gifts but should always seek to use them to further the Kingdom of God and to His glory and praise.

This same principle of good stewardship applies not only to our monetary and material possessions but also to God's other gifts to us – gifts of time, of the Holy Scriptures, of our physical bodies and of certain skills given to each of us.

The psalmist knew of the fragility of time and how short is the time we are allotted on this earth. He says, 'Remember how short my life is; remember that you created all of us mortal' (Ps. 89:47). Given this warning, it is appropriate and right that we treat time as a precious commodity, given to us by God. Therefore our response should be to make the best use of that time, to the glory of God.

As Christians we should always be thankful for the Holy Scriptures, which God has lovingly provided for us, to help us in our daily lives and to provide guidance, encouragement and support throughout all our days. It is important that we spend time studying the Scriptures and praying that the Holy Spirit will guide us as we read God's holy Word, revealing to us the meaning of that Word for us in our daily lives. It is also important that we understand our responsibility to spread the Gospel throughout the world (Matt. 28:19; 1 Cor. 9:17; Col. 1:25). Let us prayerfully seek God's guidance in how we might be effective for Him in spreading the Gospel. For example, we might undertake to support missionary work, or get involved in local evangelization through the church we are attending. Seek God's guidance for yourself in fulfilling this great commission.

We are told in Scripture that our physical bodies are given upon trust to us by God, to be used for His glory. This is another aspect of stewardship. It is important for us to understand that our bodies are given to us by God and therefore it is vital that we manage them wisely, by adopting good practices of eating and sleeping, and not abusing them through unacceptable sexual practices or use of substances such as drugs. Prayerfully read 1 Corinthians 6:12-20 and ask God to reveal to you any areas concerning your physical body that are not in accordance with His will. Remember that our bodies are 'the temple of the Holy Spirit' (1 Cor. 6:19). Let us ensure that we treat them as such.

Finally, it is important for us to understand that every Christian is given at least one gift and that we need to ensure that we use that gift or gifts to the glory of God. Holy Scripture clearly sets out this principle for our instruction in 1 Peter 3:7-11, where we are encouraged to be good managers, or stewards, of God's gifts to us. These gifts may include such things as an ability to teach adults or children about the Scriptures; serving others; visiting the sick in hospital; opening your home to others; or helping in the running of your church by being a church warden, a welcomer, a Bible reader, playing a musical instrument or being part of the choir. If you are not sure what gift or gifts God has given to you, pray about this and ask God to reveal to you what your particular gift is, and more importantly, how you might use it 'so that in all things praise may be given to God' (1 Peter 4:11).

If we always have this guiding principle at the forefront of our minds – that all we have comes from God – then it will be a great help to us as we manage our personal finances day by day. We should make this a regular request during our prayer time – that the Holy Spirit would guide us in our dealings with our personal finances, so that all our decisions and all our actions may be pleasing to God and to His glory.

Integrity
You might think that the words 'Christian' and 'integrity' go hand in hand but, sadly, this is not always the case. It is all too easy to wander from the paths of integrity in the context of managing our personal finances, and in doing so we fall short of the standards which God expects of us.

Tax returns are a very good practical example of how we should exhibit integrity in our personal finances. Legal tax avoidance schemes are acceptable but tax evasion is illegal and therefore would not be appropriate for a Christian to be involved in. Over-claiming some expenses or not declaring some income are very easy traps for us to fall into when completing our tax return. Sometimes we might think to ourselves,

'Well, other people do it so why shouldn't I?', but that is measuring ourselves against a human measuring stick which, because it is human, will almost invariably be less than it should be in terms of integrity. As Paul says, 'Do not conform yourselves to the standards of this world' (Rom. 12:2). Instead, we should be asking ourselves, 'Is this what God would want me to do?' I think that if we apply that measuring stick, then our consciences will surely guide us to be absolutely truthful in what we put on our tax return and act with integrity in all our financial dealings.

Let us hope that with King David we can say, 'Declare me innocent, O Lord, because I do what is right' (Ps. 26:1).

Let us also obey the clear mandate to all people contained in Matthew 6:33, to seek first the Kingdom of God and His righteousness. In other words, there are two overriding principles we should strive to live by. Firstly, to spread the word of the Gospel in the lives of men and women (seek first the Kingdom of God), and secondly, to live a life of holiness in the power of the Holy Spirit. Integrity is one way in which we can demonstrate to a secular world that we are striving to live a life of holiness, in obedience to God's holy Word.

Honesty

In all our dealings with our personal finances it is important to be absolutely honest at all times. Again, you would think that Christianity and honesty go hand in hand, but as wilful, fallen human beings our hearts are still naturally sinful, and we need to carefully guard them against the tricks of the Evil One, who delights in seeing us think, say and do things which are hurtful to our heavenly Father.

When we are filling out application forms for a loan or credit card, it can be very tempting to 'exaggerate' our assets and income, so that we can obtain a larger loan than we would normally have if we were absolutely truthful about our financial situation. This is not acceptable to God and it should not be acceptable to us. We should always be absolutely honest in all our personal financial dealings.

As Holy Scripture says, 'The Lord hates people who use dishonest scales. He is happy with honest weights' and 'If you are good, you are guided by honesty' (Prov. 11:1-3). Let us at all times and in all ways strive to live lives of 'all godliness and honesty', for this 'is good and pleases God our Saviour' (1 Tim. 2:2-3).

Summary

These then are some basic principles which, if allowed to rule the area of our personal finances, will help us to lead this aspect of our lives in a way which is pleasing to God. To these principles I would add one last recommendation – seek to live a simple life.

Jesus' teaching in Matthew 6:24-33 clearly shows that to live a simple lifestyle is His instruction to all people. This instruction is strengthened by the warnings about the danger of riches, both in the Gospels (Matt. 19:23-30; Mark 10:23) and in the Epistles (1 Tim. 6:9-12; James 5:1-5). If we have our value-system right we will not seek material wealth and possessions as ends in themselves. Let us take note that this very factor kept the rich young ruler out of the Kingdom (Mark 10:17-22). Instead, let us strive to live simple, holy lives in all our dealings, so that our light might shine before others; that we may bring glory to God and be known as true disciples of Christ.

Chapter 2 – The Basics

In the area of personal finances there are a few basic, practical guidelines which will apply to most, if not all, of us at some time in our lives. Our normal education teaches us things such as mathematics, science, English, history, sport and so on, but it is rare to find teaching in the basics of handling your personal finances. Often people are just left to rely on the teaching of their parents or to find their own way in this regard, and therefore I will attempt in this chapter to outline some of the basic, practical guidelines which, if followed, will help you to manage your personal finances in a sound way.

Bank Accounts
Bank accounts ultimately fall into two categories: current accounts and savings accounts. Generally

speaking, current accounts do not pay any interest on balances held in those accounts, whereas savings accounts do pay interest. It is a good idea to have both types of account because one can be used for day-to-day transactions and the other to earn some interest on any spare cash you may have.

A current account is generally used to process transactions such as writing out cheques, drawing out cash either at the bank or from a cash dispenser, paying bills electronically and paying regular payments or direct debits.

A savings account is generally used to put aside any spare cash from a current account, so that some interest can be earned on the money whilst it is in the account. A savings account can also be used to place a regular amount into in anticipation of bills and expenses to be incurred in the future. For example, a set amount can be transferred into a savings account each month to meet bills such as telephone, gas and electricity. These bills are usually payable quarterly, so each month the balance in the savings account grows and earns some interest, then when the quarterly bill is due the funds can be transferred to a current account so that the bill can be paid.

Cheque Book
A cheque book is a useful item to have, so long as it does not cost you any extra bank account fees to have one. If your bank does make an extra charge for having a cheque book, then consider if you can manage without one.

Where a cheque book can come in useful is if you want to purchase something and the person you are buying from does not accept credit cards or debit cards, and you do not have sufficient cash on your person to pay the purchase price. In these situations often a cheque will be acceptable instead.

Always remember to fill in the cheque book stub for each cheque as you write it out, so that you know whom you have paid and how much you have paid them. This will also help you when you receive your bank statement and check it back to the cheques you have written out.

Cashpoint Card

This is a plastic card which is used to obtain cash from a cash dispensing machine. Often funds can be withdrawn from either a cheque or a savings account with a cashpoint card, simply by selecting the appropriate account on the screen of the cash machine when prompted.

The card can also be used in the cash machine to find out what the balance of your account is, obtain a statement of your account covering the last few transactions and change the PIN (or Personal Identification Number) of your card. Sometimes other functions are also available, depending on the bank you have your account with and the type of machine which you are putting your card into.

A cashpoint card also sometimes doubles as what is called a debit card. A debit card allows you to pay for goods and services directly from your account, assuming the person you are buying from accepts such means of payment. The card is usually inserted into or swiped through an electronic device and the cardholder is then prompted to input their PIN. The electronic link to the bank's computer checks that there are sufficient funds in the account to meet the transaction, and that the PIN is correct, all in a matter of seconds. If everything is in order then the transaction is approved. Your account is then debited with the amount of the transaction, and the person you are buying from electronically receives the amount directly into their bank account.

Credit Card

A lot of people, and certainly a large proportion of the media, will tell you that credit cards are evil things which get people into all sorts of financial difficulties, incurring debt which they cannot hope to repay. I do not subscribe to this view. A credit card, if used properly, can be useful in helping you manage your finances to best advantage.

Note that I use the word credit card in the singular rather than the plural. There is a very good reason for this, and that is that one credit card should be sufficient for all your needs. There is no need to have multiple credit cards, and those people who do have multiple cards are often the ones who do not use them properly and responsibly.

Lots of people and the media often criticise banks and financial institutions for making it too easy for people to obtain credit on credit cards. This argument, I think, misses the point. At the end of the day it is our responsibility and ours alone to ensure that we do not borrow more than we can afford to repay. The real issue is that people who borrow on multiple credit cards do so because they want something and they want it now, rather than saving up for it. This is poor management of their finances, caused by greed. Scripture warns us against greed. In the New Testament we read, 'since you are God's people, it is not right that any matters of greed should ever be mentioned among you' (Eph. 5:3). In the Old Testament we read of Achan, who disobeyed God's command not to take from Jericho anything that was to be destroyed. Achan saw beautiful things amongst the items seized from the city, which were to be set apart for the Lord and placed in the Lord's Treasury. Achan wanted these things so much that his greed caused him to take them, and thus he brought shame and destruction upon his family (Josh. 7:20-21). Again in the Old Testament we read that God says, 'I was angry with them because of their sin and greed' (Isa. 57:17). In the New Testament, Jesus tells the parable of the rich fool and says, 'Watch out and guard yourselves from every kind of greed, because a person's true life is not made up of the things he owns, no matter how rich he may be' (Luke 12:15).

As Christians we are not exempt from the temptation of greed, or covetousness as we may call it. In fact it is one of the 'fiery darts' which the Evil One uses to cause us to slip up in our Christian walk and thus hurt our loving Father in heaven. We see a sad, but salutary, example of this in the Old Testament recounting of Lot's wife. She was a woman with many religious privileges. She was married to 'a righteous man' (2 Pet. 2:7), and her uncle by marriage was Abraham himself. She enjoyed the privilege of living within a godly family environment, which is a privilege indeed. Yet she did not know God and indeed was openly disobedient to Him. Her heart was never really set upon the things above, but coveted all the things that this secular, material world has to offer.

Lot and his wife lived in the city of Sodom, which was a worldly place, no doubt full of all the things which we may ourselves see today in our society, such as the pleasures of this world, material things, self-interest and abuse of power. Indeed, we are also told in Genesis 19 of some of the specific evils evident in Sodom, including sexual immorality, causing the Lord Himself to say, 'There are terrible accusations against Sodom and Gomorrah, and their sin is very great' (Gen. 18:20). This very sin caused the Lord to determine to destroy the cities completely, but because Lot was a righteous man, God spared him and instructed him to leave the city with his family before the destruction came upon it. God warned Lot and his family not to look back as they ran from the city, but Lot's wife coveted the things the city had to offer and did look back, in direct disobedience to the warning God had given. As a result she was immediately turned into a pillar of salt. This is a solemn and salutary lesson for us all, not to eagerly desire, or covet, the things of this world. Jesus Himself warns us of this when He says, 'Remember Lot's wife' (Luke 17:32).

In *Pilgrim's Progress*, that wonderfully instructive book by John Bunyan, we read about a place called Vanity, through which the hero, Christian, travels while on his journey to the Celestial City. The town of Vanity is the location for the Vanity Fair, a place where all manner of material things and pleasures of this world may be purchased. Christian is warned not to be beguiled by the wares of this fair and certainly not to buy anything which is for sale there. We read that Christian 'set very light by all their wares and cared not so much as to look upon them'. He turned his eyes away from them and

26

'looked upwards, signifying that his trade and traffic was in Heaven'. Let us hope that we do likewise and do not become beguiled by the things of this world for, as *Pilgrim's Progress* goes on to say, 'Christianity and the customs of the town of Vanity are diametrically opposite and cannot be reconciled'.

There are many things in this world which may tempt us to greed and covetousness, just as Achan was tempted, as Lot's wife was tempted, and as Christian was tempted, such as material possessions, nice clothes, jewellery and so on. I am not saying that it is wrong to have these things, but we must guard against the desire to give in to that temptation and seek to have them right now, which may lead us to think that we can 'put it on the credit card' and worry about paying it back later. That is how people get into financial difficulties with credit cards. There is an old saying which goes, 'If you can't afford it, don't buy it'! Or as Holy Scripture says, 'It is better to be satisfied with what you have than to be always wanting something else' (Eccles. 6:9).

If used responsibly and correctly, credit cards can be useful tools in the management of our personal finances. Firstly, most retailers accept credit cards and this means that we do not need to carry large amounts of cash on our person but can use our credit card to pay for goods and services instead. This has obvious benefits from a safety point of view. Secondly, by using credit cards correctly we can earn a little more interest on our hard-earned money, because when we buy something using our credit card it may be anything up to six weeks before the statement arrives and we need to pay it off. During that time, we can be using a savings account to earn some interest on our money. As long as we pay the credit card statement in full when it arrives, then no interest is payable to the credit card company, so we have benefited from using our credit card for purchases instead of cash. It is important to factor into the equation any annual fee payable for the credit card as this can be more than the interest you may earn over a year. Not all credit cards have an annual fee, so shop around to find the best deal. It is also important to remember that some credit cards have points schemes, where points are earned each time the card is used. These points can then be redeemed for goods and services, or vouchers which can be used at supermarkets to pay for things such as groceries.

The key thing to remember is that you should only use a credit card if you are certain you have the money to pay the statement in full when it arrives. Never leave any debt on a credit card, as the interest rates are very high and make it harder to repay that debt over time.

If you already find yourself in the position of having multiple credit card debts which you are struggling to repay, then consider applying to your bank for a personal loan to consolidate all of your debts into one loan, with repayments at a level which you can afford. I will discuss the subject of personal loans in greater detail later in this chapter. However, if you do follow this course of action, ensure that you cut up your credit cards so that you are not tempted to go straight back out there and run up additional debts. This would be a very foolish thing to do and certainly not the act of a responsible person, Christian or non-Christian. An alternative to seeking a personal loan to consolidate all of your debts might be to apply for a special deal which credit card companies sometimes offer whereby you transfer all or some of your existing credit card debt to the credit card they are offering you, but at significantly reduced interest rates than those you are currently struggling to cope with on your existing credit cards. By lowering the interest rate on all or a portion of your overall debt, this can assist you in paying it off, because the interest costs will be less. However, the same rule applies as for personal loans in that if you do take this course of action, you must ensure that you don't run up debts again on your existing credit cards. If necessary, cut up your existing credit cards to help you overcome the temptation to use them unwisely.

Monthly Bank Statement
An important part of being responsible with your personal finances is to ensure that you ask your bank for a regular bank statement, preferably monthly. It is also important that you actually do something with that statement when it arrives, and not just look at the closing balance and then file it or throw it away.

When the statement arrives, take a few moments to tick back all of the entries to your cheque book stubs, cashpoint receipts (which of course you have retained for this purpose!), salary confirmations and other evidence of payments or receipts such as electronic banking confirmations. This process is called reconciling. The aim is to ensure that all of the entries on your statement agree with what you expect them to be, and that the balance of your account is also what you expect it to be.

This process is also vital in identifying any entries on your statement which you cannot agree with. If this occurs, it is important to notify your bank straightaway so that they can look into the matter for you. If you leave it a long time before raising the issue with your bank, the likelihood of the matter being resolved satisfactorily is diminished.

Keep your bank statements for at least 5 years to comply with taxation laws and also because if you apply for a loan with a bank or other financial institution, they may ask to see your bank statements for a certain period, to ensure that you are a good manager of your finances and also to confirm what you may have written in your loan application.

Electronic Banking

Electronic banking, or as it is sometimes called, internet banking, is a useful tool to help you manage your personal finances. Of course you will need to have a home computer to be able to use this service, and also that computer will need to be connected to the internet.

Electronic banking allows you to access your bank account, pay bills, see transactions which have gone through your account, and order things such as cheque books and statements. It can be a convenient and cost-effective tool to assist you in the management of your finances, because generally the cost of an electronic payment is less than that of a cheque, plus the service is usually available 24 hours a day, 365 days a year. This means that you can do your banking in the evening or at the weekend, from the comfort of your home and without having to worry that the bank might be closed just when you want to carry out a transaction.

Often people worry about the security of electronic banking, which the media does not help by printing scare-mongering stories each time there is a problem.

The fact is that there are millions of electronic banking transactions happening every day and occasionally something goes wrong. However, if you bring it to the attention of your bank straightaway they will usually sort it out for you. There are certain precautions you can take, though, to ensure that the likelihood of anything happening to you is greatly diminished.

Firstly, never divulge your password to anyone. Husbands and wives should have their own individual passwords for accessing the system and these passwords should not be written down anywhere. Choose something which is easy to remember and commit it to memory.

Secondly, an issue to be aware of is the growing trend today of what is known as 'phishing'. This is where a person receives an email purporting to be from their bank, asking them to confirm their electronic banking details including their password. *Never respond to these requests*. They are from unscrupulous people who just want to obtain your electronic banking details in order to steal your money. Banks never ask you to divulge your password, so if you receive such a request, do not respond.

Thirdly, when you access your bank's electronic banking system, a small padlock symbol will appear on your screen, usually in the top or bottom right hand corner of your computer. Also, the web address will change from 'http' to 'https'. Both of these items indicate that you are on what is known as a secure site, which is protected from prying eyes by sophisticated security systems. Therefore, you are safe to use this site knowing that your details are secure and that no one else is gaining access to your account.

Finally, always ensure that you have anti-virus, spyware detection and personal firewall software loaded onto your computer. This will minimize the risk of someone finding out your electronic banking details and using them to steal money from your account. The software can be purchased from all good computer shops and major office supplies retailers.

Mortgages
The majority of people in the Western world, Christian and non-Christian, at some stage in their lives own their own home. When I say 'own', I of course mean that that they take out a mortgage or home loan and use this, usually together with some of their own money, to purchase a property to live in. Because of the size of mortgages, it often takes many years to fully repay the loan and thus be at a stage where they own the property outright. Generally speaking, however, a property is a sound investment which, if held for a large number of years, will hold its value and even appreciate in value.

Despite what I said earlier about only buying something if you have the cash to buy it outright, a mortgage is the exception to this rule. If we all had to save up enough money to buy a property, it is likely that we would not succeed in our lifetime! However, there are some general guidelines which should be followed when buying a property and talking out a mortgage, to avoid getting into a position of financial stress.

Firstly, never borrow more than you can comfortably afford to repay. Find out from your bank how much a mortgage will cost before you commit yourself to a purchase. Some computer programs such as Microsoft Excel, and bank websites have standard templates which enable you to insert the amount of the loan, the interest rate you will be paying (which you can also find on the bank's website), and the term of the loan (that is, how many years the loan is taken out for). Once this information is inserted, the program tells you what the repayments will be on the mortgage. Complete a budget (see Chapter 3 – Budgeting) to find out how much you can afford in mortgage repayments and compare this to the figure you have for the amount of the repayments. Always make sure that you can comfortably afford the repayments, because this will provide a safety net should you have unforeseen expenses or if interest rates should rise. If your mortgage is linked to a variable rate this means the repayments will increase if interest rates generally increase. An alternative option to consider is a fixed rate mortgage, where the interest rate is fixed for a certain term despite what happens to interest rates generally, so if interest rates rise and you have a fixed rate mortgage, then your repayments do not increase. Conversely, though, should interest rates go down you will be still on your fixed rate and your repayments will not go down. A key benefit of a fixed rate mortgage is that it provides certainty of repayment whatever the fixed rate period is. In other words, if you take out a fixed rate mortgage for three years, your repayments will stay the same for the entire three year period, irrespective of what happens to interest rates generally. This certainty can be very useful if you are on a tight budget and cannot afford for your repayments to increase above a certain amount if interest rates go up. Carefully consider all of these options when choosing a mortgage – your bank or broker should set out all the options for you so that you can make an informed decision.

Secondly, have a good margin between the amount of your mortgage and the value of your property. By this I mean borrowing no more than, for example, 80 per cent of the value of the property. Ideally, if you can borrow less than this, that would be even better. This approach provides a further safety net should the value of your property fall, which can happen when the market dips. Also, if you borrow more than 80 per cent of the value of the property you are likely to incur additional costs called 'higher lending charges', which is where a lender makes a charge if the amount of the mortgage exceeds a given percentage of the value of the property. Generally, these additional charges are avoidable by restricting yourself to borrowing a maximum of 80 per cent of the value of the property.

Ensuring that you can comfortably afford your mortgage repayments by only borrowing a maximum of 80 per cent of the value of the property might sound a bit conservative, but my experience over the years tells me that this is by far the best course of action if you want to avoid financial pressure, and the stress which goes with it.

Personal Loans

Personal loans can be used for a variety of purposes, such as purchasing a car, purchasing furniture or paying for a holiday. These examples I have quoted are chosen carefully because, whilst a car may be a necessity in order to travel to work, I would strongly advise you against borrowing money for furniture or a holiday. Taking on additional debt to acquire something which is essentially nice to have but not necessary is not a good idea because, for example, you may find that you are still paying off one loan for a holiday when the time comes that you want another holiday! In this situation you might take out another loan so you now have even more debt to repay. I am not saying that you should not have a holiday. Holidays can be an important time for rest and reflection, but I would urge you to only have a holiday which you can afford to pay for without having to borrow money.

There are times when a personal loan can be a good solution, and this is particularly so if you are already in a position where you have multiple debts on existing loans and/or credit cards. Often the total repayments on all of this debt will be high and may even be more than you can afford. One way of reducing these repayments may be to consolidate all the debts into just one personal loan, with a repayment which you can afford. If you are in this situation, enquire from your bank if it is possible to have a loan to consolidate all your other debts and how much such a loan will cost. If the bank agrees to help you they will almost certainly, and rightly so, insist that you cut up all your credit cards so that you are not tempted to go straight back out there and start running up debts again. Think about this sensibly – what is the point in running up debt which you cannot afford to repay? I guarantee that it will only cause you misery and stress and, in a worse scenario, may even force you into bankruptcy, which is a very unpleasant position to be in and may forever affect your ability to borrow any money, including potentially preventing you being able to purchase a property which you want to call your home.

Chapter 3 – Budgeting

Budgeting is arguably the most important aspect of personal finances, but it is also true to say that it is arguably the area most neglected by many people. However, let me caution you at the outset – if you do not have a proper household budget, you greatly increase your chances of getting into a financial mess and being a less than responsible steward of all that God has blessed you with.

In the sincere hope of being helpful in preventing this happening to you, let us look at some basic guidelines which, if followed, should mean that you are in much better control of your finances at all times.

What is a budget?
In its broadest sense, a budget is where you work out how much you need to spend on something or some

things in the future, and then bring that amount back to the current time and work out how much you need to be setting aside to meet the planned expenditure. Once you know how much needs to be set aside you can then work out if you actually have the money to be able to achieve everything that you want to.

An example might be a telephone bill. Let us say that your quarterly bill is likely to be in the region of £100. Because the bill is payable quarterly (that is, every 3 months) you can divide the amount of £100 by 3 to work out how much you need to set aside each month to meet the bill when it arrives. In this case, the answer is £33 (£100 divided by 3). If you set aside £33 each month then, when the telephone bill for £100 arrives, you will have the money to pay it, rather than waiting for the bill to arrive and then wondering how you are going to find the money to pay it.

If you use this same principle for all your future expenditure, you are well on the way to establishing a budget for all your financial needs.

How to budget

Using the principle set out above, you can now sit down and work out a formal budget for all your financial expenditure. An example budget is included in the Appendix at the end of this book. Have a look at that budget now and then we will work through this example.

Step 1 in preparing your budget is to list everything you will need to spend money on during the year. The list of items shown in the example is not exhaustive and also not all the items will apply to everyone, but it should get you thinking about the different things you have to pay for during the year. Make sure that you include all of the items you personally have to pay for in your own budget.

Step 2 is to fill in the monthly or quarterly cost of each item, depending on whether you pay for that item monthly or quarterly. That is why some of the items in the example have a number in the quarterly column, because they are payable quarterly.

Step 3 is to 'gross' everything up to an annual basis, either by multiplying the monthly items by 12 or the quarterly items by 4. If you had items which were payable weekly or every 6 months then you would obviously multiply by 52 or 2 respectively.

Step 4 is to bring all of the annual figures back to a monthly equivalent. For example, Water Rates are payable at the rate of £105 per quarter, so in our example the annual figure is £420 (£105 multiplied by 4). We then bring that annual figure back to a monthly equivalent, so we divide £420 by 12 to arrive at a monthly figure of £35.

If we do this for all of the items, then we now know how much we need to set aside each month to pay for all of our annual expenditure. In the example you can see that the monthly figure for total expenditure is £2,168. Compare that figure with our monthly income of £2,300 and you can see that we only have £132 left over. Therefore, it would be very foolish of us to go out, for example, and buy some furniture on hire purchase at a cost of £200 per month, because we know that this means our monthly expenditure will now exceed our monthly income.

Step 5 is to review this budget on a regular basis, at least annually, to ensure that as your expenses increase (as they inevitably will through inflationary pressures) then you always have enough 'set aside' to meet all your expenditure. If you find yourself already in the position of having more expenditure than income, then you need to carefully go through each item looking for ways in which you can reduce expenditure. Examples of how you might achieve this include shopping around for better deals on items such as insurance and telephone costs, making sandwiches to take to work each day instead of buying food at lunchtime, or considering the use of public transport instead of the car.

Saving for a rainy day

In the example used, it can be seen that we have not included any amount for what might be termed savings 'for a rainy day'. By this I mean putting aside an amount each month into a savings account so that if you receive unexpected bills or a situation occurs where you encounter unexpected expenditure on, for example, a new fridge, then you have a small reserve of funds to meet this expenditure.

This is a responsible thing to do and something I would encourage you to think about doing, because being a Christian does not mean that we will not experience unexpected expenditure requirements. For example, there is no guarantee that our household appliances will last forever. This is because they are of this world and, as with all things of this world, they decay and break down. Therefore it is important to have a small 'emergency reserve' put aside for such eventualities.

The Bible gives us examples of 'saving for a rainy day'. In the book of Genesis, chapters 37-50, we read the story of Joseph and his exile in Egypt because of the jealousy of his brothers. God blessed Joseph even though he was in prison, and Joseph interpreted dreams for the king of Egypt, causing the king to appoint Joseph as Governor over all the land. 'Your authority will be second only to mine,' said the king (Gen. 41:40). Joseph saw to it that during the years of plenty in Egypt, some of the crops and food was placed in storage rather than all being used straightaway. 'In each city he stored the food from the fields around it' (Gen. 41:48). Then when a time of famine came upon the country, Joseph ordered that the storehouses be opened and food distributed to the people so that they did not starve (Gen. 41:56). This is a great biblical example of putting aside a little so that when hard times come, we have something in reserve to call upon and help us through those hard times.

If you can't afford it, don't buy it!

It can be seen from the budgeting example that we would be foolish to incur additional expenditure on something when we do not have the income to pay for it. This rule applies whether we are purchasing something outright and don't have the cash to do it, or taking on additional debt where we cannot comfortably afford the repayments.

There is an old saying which goes 'if you can't afford it, don't buy it', and I think that the person who invented that saying had it spot on. Unfortunately, there is a common trait among people today that they see something and want it now. They are not prepared to save up for it and often will just go out and buy it on the credit card or use up all their spare cash in completing the purchase. I hope I have demonstrated above that both of these actions are foolhardy and reckless. If we go ahead and do it anyway, then there is much evidence of the wilful, fallen state of our hearts. As Jesus said, 'For from the inside, from a person's heart, come the evil ideas which lead him to do immoral things' (Mark 7:21).

If we pursue a policy of seeing something and either 'putting it on the credit card' or using all our spare cash to acquire it, whatever it is, we clearly display the sins of greed and impatience, together with a wanton disregard for the consequences of what we are doing. We are not being faithful stewards of the gift of money which God has entrusted to us.

Holy Scripture warns us against greed, for example Jesus said, 'Watch out and guard yourselves from every kind of greed' (Luke 12:15), and in the Old Testament we find that God says 'I was angry with them because of their sin and greed' (Isa. 57:17). J. C. Ryle puts it like this: 'It may be you are struggling hard for the rewards of this world. Perhaps you are straining every nerve to obtain money or place or power or pleasure. If that be your case, take care. You are sowing a crop of bitter disappointment' (J C Ryle, *Holiness*).

Scripture also tells us that patience is a thing to be valued and thus, by implication, impatience is something to be abhorred. We are told that the fruits of the Holy Spirit are 'love, joy, peace, *patience*, kindness, goodness, faithfulness, humility and self-control' (Gal. 5:22) [author's italics]. If we would be true followers of Christ and thus possessed by the Holy Spirit, then we should seek, with the Spirit's help, to overcome any impatience we may have to give in to the desire to see something and want it now, and thus embark on a foolhardy path of spending all our spare cash on that thing, or taking on extra debt just so that we can have it now.

There is a cautionary tale on this subject contained in John Bunyan's *Pilgrim's Progress*, of two children called Passion and Patience. We read that 'Passion seemed to be much discontent, but Patience was very quiet'. When the hero of the book, Christian, seeks to understand why this is, he is told that Passion wants things now and is not prepared to wait for them, while Patience is prepared to wait for them. We read further that Passion is then given treasure and is happy for a while, but soon he 'lavished all away and had nothing left him but rags'. Let us seek to be more like Patience than Passion!

Affordability versus Justification
I would like to take the argument discussed in the last section one step further and suggest that, even if we can afford something, can we justify the expense on that particular purchase? Let me give you a personal example. I am mad about cars. They are a real passion of mine and I am a regular attendee at motor shows to have a look at and sit in all the new cars which are for sale. Now I might try to convince myself there is an argument for saying that I could afford to buy a more expensive car, possibly one with a prestige badge on it. However, there is a niggling doubt in my mind about whether, as a Christian, I can justify that expenditure on such a material item, and one which almost certainly will cost me a lot of money, not only in its initial purchase but in the loss of value it will incur as it gets older and does more mileage. If I stop to think about how I might better spend that money to glorify God, then the argument within me switches from one

of affordability to justification. Perhaps the money would be better spent on supporting our church, or supporting missionary work, or both?

There is no doubt that this question is a very personal one, and one which only you can answer. All I would ask is that you seek prayerfully to understand which course of action you should take when faced with such decisions. Remember that 'Much is required from the person to whom much is given; much more is required from the person to whom much more is given' (Luke12:48). If God has blessed us with material wealth, then there is a greater responsibility to be considerate and careful in how we use that wealth.

Chapter 4 – Investing

People invest money for a number of reasons. Some just want to make more money. This is something I would not advocate for Christians. Let us not be like the seed which fell among the thorns, where 'the love for riches…crowd in and choke the message, and they don't bear fruit' (Mark 4:19).

However, some people need to invest to provide for their retirement or to provide an additional income stream to supplement their retirement income. For some people, investment income may even be their only source of income, so they need to be successful at it in order to generate sufficient income for their daily needs.

Some people may argue that investing is something Christians shouldn't do, because it is likened to gambling. Let me clear this matter up first before setting out some basic guidelines on investing.

By investing I mean the act of putting money into 'something', for example shares or property, with a view to getting back what has been invested plus an additional amount. I can understand that on the face of it this might be interpreted as the same thing as putting money into a slot machine, or betting on the outcome of a horse race – money is 'invested' with a view to getting back winnings which will exceed the amount 'invested'. However, there is a significant difference between the latter, which I would more correctly call gambling, and the former, which I would call investing.

The main difference is that with gambling the likelihood of obtaining a return is based purely on 'luck'. Horse racing punters might argue that they have a 'system' for choosing which horse to back, but this argument does not stack up simply on the grounds that I have not met anyone who consistently wins by backing horses, and that ultimately they lose money. The same argument goes for any form of gambling, be it horse racing, slot machines, card games or lottery tickets. You only have to speak to organizations such as Gamblers Anonymous and they will tell you that gamblers always lose in the end.

Investing should never be based purely on 'luck'. It is the considered investing of money into something which has a proven track record of delivering returns to the investor. If you go back ten, fifteen, twenty or twenty-five years, it has been shown that the returns from the stock market and returns from property have been positive; that is, the investor has received back their original investment (or capital) plus an additional amount. Many Christians are working as fund and investment managers throughout the world, and through their skill and knowledge they have, over time, successfully invested money on behalf of their clients. This is not gambling – it is the considered investment of money by professional people in something which has provided their customers with a reasonable return on their investment.

Let us be absolutely clear on this. Gambling is something which is inappropriate for Christians to engage in. We only need look around at people we know or have heard about who take part in gambling. It is destructive to the people themselves and to those around them such as family and friends. It is absolutely wrong for Christians to gamble.

Where the line between gambling and investing becomes slightly blurred is where, for example, someone invests money into shares when they have insufficient knowledge about what they are doing or what they are investing in. This is, to my mind, closer to gambling than it is investing and as such should be avoided at all times. Equally, if someone invests money into a project without fully understanding what they are investing in or the risks involved, then again this is more akin to gambling than investing and should be avoided.

Risk versus Return

Let me mention an old adage here, which will serve you well if you are thinking of investing in something. The saying goes: 'If it sounds too good to be true, then it probably is!'

Let me explain further. Investing involves the tried and trusted theory of risk versus return. The theory is that the higher the return being sought, then the higher the risk. Conversely, the lower the return, the lower the risk. Therefore, if someone is promising you an exceptional return with little or no risk, I would caution you to seek professional advice before investing your money. If a high return is being promised, you can be assured that the risk of you losing your money is also high, despite what any advertising material or salesperson might say to the contrary.

So, how do you know where the line is between little risk and higher risk? Well, as a general rule of thumb, have a look at what the central bank interest rate is at the present time. Generally, that same rate will equate to the investment of little risk, such as bank deposits or government bonds. The greater the difference between that rate and the rate of return being promised by your investment, the greater the risk is of you losing some or all of your original capital. For example, I have seen over the years investments promising returns of 10 per cent or more when the central bank rate is 5-6 per cent. Sometimes also the advertising material for those investments, to my mind, leaves a lot to be desired in terms of making the risks absolutely clear to an investor. People invest their money thinking it is a safe and secure investment, only to find out when the company fails that their investment is not so safe and secure after all, and they lose everything they have invested. So beware if an investment is being sold to you as low or no risk and the promised return is significantly above the central bank rate at the time. In practice, this will simply not be the case.

To most people, investments mean things like shares and property, and for the sake of keeping things simple, those are the sorts of investments we will look at in this book. But first let us have a look generally at how risky these types of investments are and what return the investor can expect from them, bearing in mind what we have already said about risk versus return, and that the higher the return the higher the risk.

Cash deposits are generally classed as low risk and therefore the returns will also be relatively low. Whatever the central bank rate is at any given time will provide a good idea of the rate of return offered by cash deposits. For example, if the central bank rate is 5 per cent then an investor can expect to receive, at best, 5 per cent or thereabouts.

Moving up the risk scale, and looking at the general categories of investments mentioned above, property is arguably the next category in terms of risk and return. By property I mean the direct purchasing of a property and not investing in a property investment fund. In general an investor can expect a return from property that is in excess of that received from cash deposits, but also the risk is higher than with cash deposits. In particular, property investments need to be held for the medium to long term, that is 5 years plus, to achieve a return which is acceptable for the risk involved. Property values do go down as well as up, so the longer the property is held, the greater the likelihood of any reductions in value being more than offset by increases in value. Also, when choosing a property it is important to do your homework – research the area you are considering investing in and what prices are like in that area. Generally, areas with good transport links, or close to favoured schools, are always going to be in demand and thus are perhaps a safer investment than areas without these features. Remember also to factor into your investment decision the cost of maintaining the property, such as rates, repairs and maintenance costs, heat, light and power.

The next class of investment, shares, probably ranks as the most risky which we will look at in this book. Of course, because the risk is higher the investor can also expect higher returns, and because, generally, shares will over time outperform cash deposits and property as an investment. I say 'over time' because shares can be very volatile investments and can go down just as quickly as they can go up. However, over the medium to long term it has been shown that shares generally outperform cash deposits and property.

How much risk you are prepared to take when investing is a personal thing and I would not presume to tell you what you should do or not do. All I would say is that if you feel uncomfortable with an investment, then either learn more about it until you feel more comfortable, or stay away from it altogether.

We will now have a look at the different forms of investment in more detail.

Cash Deposits
These are savings accounts offered by a wide range of banks, building societies and other financial institutions. Generally speaking, they are a safe form of investment as long as you choose a reputable institution. If you have access to a computer, have a look at websites which compare what savings accounts are available and the current rates of interest they are paying.

Some savings accounts are operated purely as 'online' accounts. That is, you can only access the balance electronically, transferring funds to and from your current account as you need to. Often these accounts pay a higher rate of interest because they are less expensive to administer from the institution's perspective. If you feel comfortable using a computer, then this type of account should be considered.

There are also accounts available known as term deposits. This is where your money is 'locked in' for a term of your choice, which can be anywhere between 7 days and 12 months. The interest rate offered by the institution is guaranteed for the period of the deposit, with interest generally paid when the deposit matures at the end of the agreed term. These can be useful if you want to have certainty over the rate of return, or interest rate, paid. Once you have invested your money the rate is guaranteed, and even if interest rates generally go down, you will still receive the agreed rate. Conversely, if interest rates generally go up after you have invested your money, then you will be locked in at the rate already agreed for the term deposit. This is one of the disadvantages of this type of investment, together with the fact that once you have invested, you cannot access your money until the agreed maturity date, without incurring a penalty. These factors need to be fully considered before making an investment decision.

Because savings accounts are considered low risk, the return you will obtain on your money is also relatively low. You would not expect to receive a rate of interest much in excess of the central bank rate current at that time. Anything that purports to be a savings account and offers a return well above the central bank rate should be treated with caution – it is likely to be something different to a savings account and also carry with it a greater risk of you losing some or all of your money.

Property

As we have explored earlier, property is generally a more risky investment than cash deposits, but then the returns can also be higher.

Investing in property can take many forms. Purchasing your own home not only provides shelter for you and your family but also can be a useful investment over time. The value of the property should grow steadily, and as you pay off any loan you have on the property, your equity – that is the difference between the value of the property and the amount you owe on your mortgage – increases.

Some people purchase a second home. Often this will be located in a place which they enjoy visiting and may possibly be in a place of natural beauty, such as close to the beach or in a mountainous area. This type of property might be called a holiday home. Alternatively, sometimes the property may be located close to their place of work so that a person can stay there during the week and then return to their main home at weekends. In both cases the property is purchased for their own use and not rented out to tenants. Again, the hope is that the value of the property goes up over time so that it ends up being worth more than it was originally purchased for.

Some people purchase a property with the intention of renting it out to other people, and thus deriving an income from the rent which is paid by the tenant. The purchaser hopes to not only gain from the growth in the value of the property but also from the rental income it generates.

As already mentioned, property investments need to be held for the medium to long term, that is, five years plus, to achieve an acceptable return. Property values can go down as well as go up so it is important to do your homework and purchase property in the right location. There is a saying that there are three things to consider when purchasing property – location, location and location! Remember also that owning property brings with it the cost of maintaining that property, as mentioned earlier, so you need to bear this in mind too before deciding to invest your money in a property.

Shares
In the context of shares I am going to refer solely to shares in public companies; that is, those shares which are quoted on world stock exchanges and which are freely tradable on those stock exchanges. Such shares, because they are quoted on stock markets, have a higher degree of scrutiny and availability of investor information than other shares, and as such offer a higher degree of protection to the investor. It is possible to own shares in non-public companies, but these often carry significantly higher risk and should be avoided by the general investor.

Shares constitute the owning of a portion, or share, in a company. The value of the shares can be found easily by looking on the stock exchange where the shares are listed.

Some people might think that investing in shares is a form of gambling and, as already stated earlier in this book, if they have little or no knowledge of investing then I would agree with them. Investing directly in shares can be very risky for the unwary or uninformed and should only be done if you are confident that you know what you are doing.

However, what about those people who want to, or need to, invest in shares to get a good return, but don't know much about the subject? Well, there are a couple of options open to those people, which carry less risk than investing directly:

1. Employ the services of a stockbroker. A stockbroker is someone who is trained to invest in shares. They spend all their time analysing companies and deciding which are good investments and which are not. They advise clients on the purchase and sale of shares and receive a fee for doing so. Stockbrokers do not always get it right and, undoubtedly, there are good stockbrokers and not so good stockbrokers. If you are looking for a stockbroker, ask your trusted friends if they know of one and if that person has performed well for them. Personal recommendation is always the best way of sorting the good stockbrokers from the not-so-good ones! As mentioned, stockbrokers charge for their services, but hopefully the returns they generate for you will more than offset the cost of employing them.

2. Invest in a managed fund, or a pension fund. These funds are professionally managed and their objective is to invest money on behalf of their customers to generate a reasonable return over time. The investments made by a large number of investors are 'pooled' together and then invested by professional funds managers in shares (or other more specialised types of investments which are outside the scope of this book). The larger amount thus generated allows the fund manager to obtain a better price for the shares than an individual can obtain, and therefore the individual investors

benefit from the performance of the entire fund. Remember that the value of these funds can go down as well as up, and that is why it is important to view this type of investment as a long term strategy; that is, ten years or more.

The late Canon Leon Morris, former Principal of Ridley College, Melbourne, Australia, was an astute investor in shares. As a result, the Leon and Mildred Morris Foundation benefits from this astute knowledge, and thus helps many good causes. Canon Morris was known throughout the Christian world as a careful, conservative biblical scholar, and he clearly used his stock market astuteness to benefit others via The Morris Foundation. Investing in shares is not therefore to be seen as something inherently bad. If you know what you are doing, shares can be a valuable addition to an investment portfolio. Ultimately, it is the motivation and intent of what you are doing which is important, not the mere fact that you are investing in shares.

One last note regarding shares. As a Christian you may feel that it is inappropriate for you to invest in something which you consider to be wrong, such as tobacco companies, or armaments manufacturers, or pharmaceutical companies which carry out testing on animals. If you feel that to invest in such a company would be wrong, then be aware that there are what are called 'ethical investment' funds available to investors. These funds set out clear policies on what they will and will not invest in, and you may feel more comfortable investing in one of these funds than a more general fund which may invest in areas which you feel are not appropriate for you.

Don't have all your eggs in one basket!
This is an old saying but one which is very pertinent when looking at different types of investments.

The theory of a good investment portfolio is to have your investments spread around a range of different types of investment. By this I don't mean investing all of your money in the shares of different companies, because that would mean that you are still investing in one class of investment – shares. What I mean is spreading your money around different classes of investment so that you perhaps have some in cash deposits, some in property and some in shares (perhaps via a pension scheme). This gives your portfolio a greater balance, both from a risk point of view as you have a mix of low, medium and high risk investments, and also from a return point of view as you have a mix of low, medium, and higher return investments. The amount which you have in each class will depend on issues such as:

- Your attitude to risk – are you comfortable putting a portion of your money at risk in order to obtain a greater return?

- Your need for a higher return – if your investments have to generate a certain return in order to meet your daily needs, then you will almost certainly have to consider investing some money in higher risk classes of investments, such as shares, in order to generate higher returns.

- Have you any major expenditure coming up soon? If so, it would be very unwise to invest that money in property or shares, which can be volatile in the short term. It would be better to keep the required amount in a savings account or a term deposit account (with the term ending before the time you need the funds).

Investing can be a complex area. The above notes are intended to provide you with a broad understanding of the different types of investments and theories such as risk versus return. If you feel at all unsure about what to do, you should seek professional help from a financial advisor. Again, ask your friends if they know of one who has done a good job for them so that you hopefully receive advice from the right person. However, the above notes should help you when talking to an advisor, as you will better understand what they are talking about and this will help you to make more informed decisions.

Borrowing to Invest

There is a popular notion circulating today that people should borrow money, often against the security of their home, to invest. The fact that this notion is perpetuated by financial institutions and paid financial advisors should tell you that it is in their interests to have you follow their advice!

The rationale of borrowing to invest is that you can, using your property or existing investments as security, take on additional debt which is then invested in something – perhaps another property, shares or pension fund.

In theory, the investment earns a rate of return which exceeds the cost of the borrowed money, thereby enabling you to have investments which you would not have had if you decided not to borrow to invest.

Does this last sentence sound familiar? Have a look back at the section on credit cards in Chapter 2. Remember the cautionary tale about borrowing on a credit card simply so that you can have something now and not have to wait or save up for it? In a way, borrowing to invest is very similar. It is borrowing money so that you can have the investment now, rather than saving up for it.

I would caution everyone against borrowing to invest. Bear in mind that the rate of return the investment achieves needs to exceed the rate of interest on the borrowed money; otherwise the cost of the borrowed money will simply eat up all of the investment return. Also, the borrowed money needs to be funded out of your income. In other words, by taking on additional debt, you will incur repayments on the loan which have to be funded from your monthly, fortnightly or weekly income. If for any reason your income ceases, perhaps through ill health or accident, how are you going to meet the repayments on the loan?

I know that many people, particularly those in the financial services industry, may argue in favour of borrowing to invest; but then, of course, they would, as they benefit from you doing so. I still firmly believe that borrowing to invest places additional financial pressure and risk on a person or family which does not justify the supposed benefits. Therefore I would caution you most strongly against taking on additional debt with the aim of placing that money into some form of investment vehicle.

Chapter 5 – Retirement Planning

Some Christians might ask, 'Do I need to plan for my retirement or should I just trust God to provide for my needs?' This is a good and fair question. My wife and I have Christian missionary friends who are working in a faith mission; that is, one where they do not receive a salary but are completely dependent on the financial and prayerful support of their home church and friends for their needs. They trust God implicitly to provide for all their needs, now and in the future, and God has been faithful to them in meeting their needs – praise be to Him.

I admire these friends for their faith and commitment, and admit that my own faith is seriously lacking when compared to theirs. However, our friends received a very strong and clear call from God to join this mission and in doing so they are a great encouragement and example to me of God's faithfulness and love, as well as being faithful workers for Him in that mission.

Not everyone is called to be a missionary worker and many Christians find themselves in a secular workplace. I don't see this necessarily as a negative thing because we can be powerful witnesses for God in the workplace, just as we can in the mission field. How we behave, what we say and what we do can all bring glory to God, and in so doing let us pray that our work colleagues will see in us something different and give us the opportunity to share our faith with them. There is a very good book on this subject called *Secular Work is Full Time Service* by Larry Peabody (published by Christian Literature Crusade). I thoroughly recommend this book to you if you have the opportunity to get your hands on a copy.

Let me at this stage draw a distinction between *planning* for our financial situation in retirement and *worrying* about our financial situation in retirement. The Bible tells us clearly, 'Do not worry about tomorrow; it will have enough worries of its own' (Matt. 6:34). So do not worry about your future financial situation when you retire, but at the same time do not just ignore it altogether. I firmly believe that God has given us a brain and fully expects that we should use that brain during our lives on this earth. One aspect of how we use our brains is in managing our personal finances and in particular how we plan for the future, to provide for our families throughout our entire lifetime, including retirement.

For most people, Christians and non-Christians alike, they will have a period of their lives where they are working and earning money. Then, when they reach a certain age they will stop working, perhaps through choice or declining health. Unfortunately, our household bills do not stop at the same time, so we need to ensure that we plan for that eventuality by putting aside funds during our working days, in order to provide an income in our retirement. This is called retirement planning.

Let me say at the outset, I fully understand that some governments provide a state pension at retirement to the majority of people living in that country. However, it is true to say that the real value of that pension has fallen over the years, and as the demographic make-up of those countries changes, with people living longer and starting work later, the pressures on government schemes will grow. Therefore, it would, in my opinion, be unwise to rely solely on the Government to provide for you in retirement – you need to take matters into your own hands and plan ahead.

The most common way that people plan for their retirement financially is to have a pension scheme. Simply put, this is an investment fund which you contribute to throughout your working life and which then provides an income for you in retirement. Most people invest in schemes which are professionally managed and, hopefully, run by reputable companies. The company receives money from you and all the other investors in the scheme, and then invests that money on behalf of the investors in a range of investments, such as cash, government bonds, shares and property. When you retire you usually have the option of taking a lump sum of money plus a regular income, or just a regular income. Obviously, if you opt not to take a lump sum, then the regular income portion will be greater than if you did take a lump sum, because you are using the entire value of your scheme to generate an income rather than having a value which has been reduced by the amount of your lump sum. There are occasions when people opt to take the lump sum anyway, because, for example, they want to pay off their mortgage, or want to take an overseas trip, but bear in mind that if you do this then the amount you receive as a regular income will be reduced.

It is important to start contributing to your pension scheme as soon as possible, because you then maximise the number of years the fund has to grow. If the investment managers do their job well, then the fund should grow each year, and obviously the more years that it has to grow, the greater will be the value of the fund when you come to retire. If you leave it until a few years before retirement to contribute to your scheme, then it clearly does not have much opportunity to grow.

Another thing to consider is which type of fund you want your contributions to go into. Most pension companies offer a range of funds from low risk, through medium risk, to higher risk. In the earlier years of your fund it will probably be advisable to opt for a medium or higher risk strategy because, as we have already said, the higher the risk the higher the return, and you want to maximize your return over the majority of the years your fund is invested. However, as you near retirement it would be advisable to switch into a lower risk option so that your fund is protected against any major fluctuations just when you want to get your hands on it! Most pension companies do not charge for switching fund options, as long as you do not do it too often.

How much should I be contributing to a pension scheme?
This is an important question and, in a sense, you have to start at the end and work back from there. That probably sounds silly but what I mean is that you need to work out what level of income you will require at retirement before you can work out how much to contribute now.

For the purposes of the exercise you can ignore the impact of inflation and simply ask yourself, if you retired today, what level of income you would need to cover all of your outgoings. Bear in mind things like your mortgage, which you may have paid off by the time you retire so you do not need to include any repayments in your calculations. Use the budgeting instructions in Chapter 3 to help you work out what level of income you need.

Once you have worked out how much you need, have a look at the websites of various pension companies. Most now have a built-in calculator where you enter what level of income you require and when you intend to retire, and the system automatically calculates how much you need to be putting aside now to meet those requirements. It can sometimes be a bit of a shock when you see the figure, particularly if you are relatively close to retirement age, but this just underlines what I have already said, that the earlier you can start contributing to a scheme, the better it will be when you retire and want to access your fund.

Alternatively, as a very rough rule of thumb and assuming that you are aged 40 or under, you should try to put a minimum of 10 per cent of your income into a pension scheme. If you are over 40 and have not already got much in your scheme then you may have to consider contributing well in excess of 10 per cent in order to have a reasonable fund when you come to retire and need to draw on that fund. The reason for this goes back to what I said earlier about the need to start contributing to a fund as early as you can, to give the fund the maximum length of time to grow through its investment returns.

Chapter 6 – Protecting Your Family

In this world you only have to look around to see that there are times when financial hardship falls on a family. This might be due to the loss of a loved one, the onset of a serious illness, a serious accident causing permanent disability, or if you are self-employed, a less serious accident but one which still prevents you from working for a while and thus not earning any income.

As Christians we are not exempt from such events. Let us know that following Jesus will not prevent us having earthly sorrows and troubles. Jesus Himself teaches us that even though we may be a servant of His, we may have to endure anxiety and pain. He tells the disciples, 'You will indeed drink the cup I must drink and be baptized in the way I must be baptized' (Mark 10:39). In saying this Jesus was pointing to the fact that they (His disciples) would be killed by men, just as He would be killed. We also read in the Bible about Stephen, who was stoned to death for being a follower of Jesus (Acts 7:59), and of Paul, who was stoned at Lystra (Acts 14:19), imprisoned at Philippi (Acts 16) and eventually killed in Rome in A.D. 67 for preaching the Good News of Jesus Christ. In the Old Testament we read in the wonderfully encouraging Psalm 23: 'Even though I go through the deepest darkness, I will not be afraid, Lord, for you are with me' (Ps. 23:4). It is clear from this psalm that we will experience sorrows and times of trouble in this world. The psalm does not say that we will not go through such troubles, or that the 'valley of darkness' does not exist. What we are told, though, is that our loving Lord will be with us all the way, He will not leave us to travel the path alone, and in this we can take great hope and encouragement.

In summary, therefore, let us not be in any doubt – being a Christian does not exempt us from sickness, bereavement or ill health.

Just as our heavenly Father cares for us, His children, so should we seek to follow His example and exercise care for our families. In the context of this chapter, therefore, it is a matter of being responsible for your family in the event of death or illness affecting you or your spouse, and there are a number of strategies you can employ to help protect your family in the event of such hardship. Imagine what it would be like to have to find the mortgage repayment each month, pay the electricity and gas bills, and pay for food and clothes if your family suddenly loses one or both of its incomes. There are not many families these days who can afford to survive on just one income, and government assistance may be difficult to claim because, even if only a fairly modest amount of assets is held, this may be enough to preclude you from financial support.

Individually, or collectively, the following strategies will help pay those essential household expenses when difficult times come.

Life Assurance
Life assurance in its broadest sense means taking out a contract or policy which pays a lump sum of money to a named person, or to your estate, in the event of your death.

Consider a situation where you die and leave your spouse or partner with a large mortgage still outstanding, possibly together with credit card debts or personal loans. How is your spouse or partner going to afford the repayments on that debt now that your income is no longer contributing to the household budget?

Also, if you have children, consider that in order for your spouse or partner to work to generate income for the household, they may have to employ childcare to help look after the children while they go out to work. That childcare will cost money at a time when your household has just lost one income, putting a further strain upon the already stretched financial resources.

Taking out a life assurance policy can help in this situation by providing a lump sum of money at this difficult time, which can be used to repay some or all of that debt or at least ease some of the financial burden of meeting the repayments. Alternatively it can be used to fund childcare while the surviving spouse or partner goes out to work.

Life assurance is relatively inexpensive, but becomes more expensive as you get older. Think about how much cover you need, by considering the size of your mortgage and other debts, what income your spouse or partner earns (if any), the ages of your children, the cost of school holiday care if your children are of school age, and whether full-time childcare would be needed if anything happened to you. This will give you a starting point for then obtaining quotes from life assurance companies or an insurance broker.

Critical Illness Insurance

This type of insurance is designed to pay out a lump sum of money in the event that you are diagnosed with a serious illness such as cancer or multiple sclerosis, or that you suffer a serious heart attack which prevents you from working again. Usually the money is paid out upon diagnosis of the illness. Even if you survive the illness the money is still yours – it does not need to be paid back to the insurance company.

Similar to the example above under 'Life Assurance', consider the amount of debt you have and other financial commitments, and obtain quotations from insurance companies and insurance brokers for the amount you need to relieve your family from the financial difficulties they may face if this event happens.

Total and Permanent Disability Insurance

This is a form of insurance which, as its name suggests, pays out a lump sum of money in the event of you suffering a total and permanent disability. The insurance companies usually define this as, for example, loss of a limb, eye, or total loss of hearing due to an accident, or becoming a paraplegic or losing the use of limbs permanently.

Some insurance companies 'bundle' this insurance together with life assurance, giving you the option of having both forms of cover in one policy or opting to have just one type of cover.

As with the earlier examples of insurance, consider the amount you and your family would need in the event that you were no longer able to work because of a disability; or if you had to have a period of rehabilitation before commencing what may be part-time work or lower paid work than before.

Income Protection Insurance

This type of insurance relates mainly to those people who are self-employed, and where they do not have an employer who will continue to pay them if they have an accident and are not able to work for a period of time.

As the name suggests, the insurance policy provides an income to you in the event that you are not able to work for various reasons. The insurance companies usually stipulate that the cover is for events such as breaking a leg or arm, where you may not be able to work for a period while the injury is healing. Obviously if you are self-employed, when you cannot work you do not get paid, so it is an important insurance to consider if you have ongoing household expenses to pay, irrespective of whether you are earning any money or not.

The above details about these various types of insurance are intended to be a general guide only and insurance companies and insurance brokers will provide you with more information, and quotations, upon request. However, my intention in setting out the above is to start you thinking about being responsible and providing for your family in the event of something happening to you or your spouse.

A Final Word

Before we leave this chapter on protecting your family, I think it is appropriate for me to provide some guidance on matters which will make it easier for a surviving spouse or partner to manage the family financial situation in the event of the death of their loved one.

Firstly, it is important for both spouses or partners to have a full understanding of the financial situation of the entire family. Over my years as a bank manager I have unfortunately seen many occasions where a spouse or partner has died and the surviving spouse or partner has no clue as to what the family financial situation is, or how to access funds to keep paying household bills. This causes further unnecessary distress at a difficult time, and it can be avoided if both spouses or partners have a full understanding of their combined financial position. Therefore, make sure that both parties know where all the bank accounts are domiciled and how to pay bills such as electricity, gas and telephone. Also, both parties should look at the regular bank statement and know how much money the family has in its bank accounts, and how much is owed on any loans such as personal loans, credit cards and mortgages.

Secondly, it is important for both spouses or partners to have some financial independence. By this I mean that each spouse or partner should have their own bank account and their own credit card. This is vital if each party is to understand how financial matters are handled and thus they will be in a much better situation to cope in the event of the loss of their spouse or partner. However, it is still important that both parties share the management of the overall financial situation of the family and are open with each other about what accounts they have and how much is in those accounts.

Whilst I would advocate each party having their own bank account, I would also suggest that these accounts are held in joint names, and merely agree between yourselves whose account is whose. The reason for this is that under Common Law, if a bank account is held in joint names and one party dies, then usually the account balance automatically passes to the survivor and the account can continue to be operated as before. However, if an account is held in a sole name and that person dies, then the account will usually be frozen and the funds in the account unable to be accessed until all the legal formalities of the estate can be sorted out, which can take months. Clearly this could potentially cause a lot of financial stress if all the family funds are tied up in the frozen account.

Chapter 7 – Other Matters

In this final chapter we will explore some of the other more general questions Christians may ask, or may be exposed to, in regard to their finances and financial situation.

The love of money

There is a perception amongst some Christians that 'money is the root of all evil' and that money is inherently evil and wrong. Let us be clear that this is a mis-interpretation of Holy Scripture. The quotation comes from Paul's first letter to Timothy, chapter 6 verse 10, but what the apostle actually says is that 'the *love* of money is the root of all evil'. The key word is love.

Love is probably the most powerful emotion and force we experience in our human lives. God loved us so much that He sent His only Son to die for us 'so that everyone who believes in Him many not die but have eternal life' (John 3:16). When we love someone we spend the majority of our time and energy thinking about that person. Similarly, when we love something we spend the majority of our time and energy thinking about that 'thing', whatever it may be. So it is with money. If we love money it will be the thing we think about most – how we increase our amount of it, how we make sure we keep what we have, how we can enjoy ourselves spending it, and so on. We need only look around us today, in this increasingly material world, to see how much people love money. The same was true in biblical times, for we remember how Judas betrayed Jesus for thirty pieces of silver. Judas' love of money caused him to betray Jesus to people who Judas knew wanted to get rid of Him. He must have known that Jesus would suffer greatly and possibly even die (as He did) at the hands of His enemies, but still his love for money overcame all other thought and consideration.

Holy Scripture makes it clear that we 'cannot serve both God and money.' These words are found in Matthew 6:24 and are repeated in Luke 16:13. We can be assured that when a biblical passage is repeated it carries special significance, so the fact that this passage is repeated in both gospels should make us sit up and take extra notice. The same passage also says 'No one can be the slave of two masters – he will hate one and love the other; he will be loyal to one and despise the other'. These are powerful words and should strike a warning in our hearts to be careful about how we treat money. Scripture makes it abundantly clear that we cannot love both money and God, and that if we choose to love money then we will be turning our backs on God.

In addition, Holy Scripture makes it clear that the love of money can never be ultimately satisfying. 'If you love money, you will never be satisfied' (Eccles. 5:10). True satisfaction comes from having a real and living relationship with the Lord Jesus. Jesus said, 'I am the bread of life. He who comes to Me will never be hungry; he who believes in Me will never be thirsty' (John 6:35). We will only be fully satisfied when we humbly come to the cross of Jesus, acknowledge our sins and accept Him as our personal Saviour and Lord.

In summary, it is not money itself which is evil; it is the *love* of money which is to be abhorred. God blesses us with money for food, clothes and shelter, and intends that we should enjoy these blessings and be thankful for them. However, let us be careful not to let our wilful human hearts tend us towards the love of money, for that will be our undoing and will cause us to 'wander away from the faith' and 'break [our] hearts with many sorrows' (1 Tim. 6:10) .

Become a Christian and be wealthy!
Sadly, there are some churches today preaching this message to their unsuspecting flock. They can cite as their biblical references passages which speak of the prosperity of the righteous, such as Psalms 36:8; 37:11; 75:10; 84:11; and Proverbs 3:2. In doing so I fear that they are only telling people half the story, and therefore not presenting the full message that God intends us to receive through His holy Word. This is a dangerous thing to do, as God never intends that we 'pick and choose' the bits of the Bible we like and ignore the bits that make us feel uncomfortable. It is important to seek the complete balanced message and instruction that

the Bible gives us, to help us in our daily walk with God and in our Christian lives here on this earth.

When churches preach a message of wealth and prosperity through faith in Jesus, that message probably makes those whom they are preaching to feel happy and good about themselves. However, there is a real danger of leading these people astray from the complete truth of Holy Scripture. On numerous occasions the Bible also warns of the dangers of prosperity (Deut. 6:10-15; Prov. 30:8; Luke 6:24;12:16; James 5:1) and how it can be an easy trap for the unwary to fall into – a trap which can lure us away from God and the sort of lives He wants us to lead.

In John Bunyan's *Pilgrim's Progress* we read of the character called Hopeful, who tells of his life before becoming a Christian, when he delighted in 'all the treasures and riches of the World', those things which he says 'I believe now would have (had I continued in them still) drowned me in perdition and destruction'. We can see, therefore, that a life seeking wealth and prosperity is not the life of the true believer. The true believer does not desire these things.

Remember also the cautionary message of the rich young man who came to Jesus and asked, 'What must I do to receive eternal life?' (Mark 10:17; Matt. 19:16; Luke 18:18). The fact that this message is repeated in three gospels should tell us that it has special significance. This was a rich young man who exhibited all the signs of living a Christian life. He knew the Commandments (Mark 10:19; Luke 18:20), and he obeyed them (Mark 10:20; Matt. 19:20; Luke 18:21). Yet when Jesus replied to his question by instructing him to 'Sell all you have and give the money to the poor'

(Mark 10:21; Matt. 19:21; Luke 18:22), the rich young man went away sad because he was very rich. Jesus went on to say to His disciples, 'It is much harder for a rich person to enter the Kingdom of Heaven than for a camel to go through the eye of a needle' (Mark 10:25; Matt. 19:24; Luke 18:25).

Now Jesus didn't say it was *impossible* for a rich person to enter the Kingdom of Heaven, just harder. He wasn't saying that it was wrong for the man to be rich, but He knew the man's heart, as He knows all our hearts, and He knew that the man loved his riches more than he loved God. That was why Jesus challenged him to give away all his riches and follow Him, but the rich man was unwilling to give up his wealth and so went away sad.

Let us fully understand that wealth does not bring ultimate happiness. Studies show that even people who have won large sums of money enjoy only a temporary feeling of increased happiness, and that they soon return to the level of happiness they had before they won all that money. This has a lot to do with the fact that once we have attained a higher level of wealth or prosperity our aspirations very quickly catch up with that new level and we once again experience the need for more. Psychologists call this trait 'adaptation'. In other words we quickly adapt to our new found position of wealth and come to take it for granted. How much this sounds like the wise words of 'The Preacher' in Ecclesiastes, who wrote, 'It is all useless. It is like chasing the wind' (Eccles. 2:26).

A further cautionary message is to be found in the Old Testament. 'A working man may or may not have enough to eat but at least he can get a good night's sleep. A rich man, however, has so much that he stays awake worrying' (Eccles. 5:12). Would you prefer to be able to sleep rather than lying awake worrying? Then do not covet wealth and riches. Let us ensure that we do not love riches more than we love God. It is vital to get our hearts right before God, and we can only do this through His grace and mercy in sending His only son, Jesus Christ, to bear upon His body our sins; to take upon Himself the punishment which should be ours. If we truly understand what God has done for us by sending His son to die upon the Cross, then we will want to please God in all that we do, and live lives which are pleasing to Him. We should constantly seek the guidance of the Holy Spirit as we seek to grow in the Lord, and bring to God in prayer all areas of our lives. This includes the area of our personal finances. We should not be praying for more money and material possessions, but seeking God's will in how we deal with our personal finances, to His praise and glory.

If you are not yet a Christian but want to become one, I implore you not to do so simply because you think it will make you wealthy and prosperous. As J. C. Ryle says, 'Beware of following Christ from any secondary motive, to please relations and friends, to keep in with the custom of the place or family in which you reside, to appear respectable and have the reputation of being religious. Follow Christ for His own sake, if you follow Him at all' (J. C. Ryle, *Holiness*).

Now some Christians may ask, 'Does this mean that we as Christians are not to have nice things or financial security?' The apostle Paul says that God 'generously gives us everything for our enjoyment' (1 Tim. 6:17), but at the same time, and in the very same verse, he adds, 'Command those who are rich in the things of this life not to be proud, but to place their hope not in such an uncertain thing as riches, but in God…'(1 Tim. 6:17). There is nothing wrong with taking pleasure in the good things of this life. We should do so with thanksgiving and praise to the One 'from whom all blessings flow'. However, we need to always be mindful and prayerful of the pitfalls which prosperity can bring, and always be seeking God's will and guidance for this area of our lives.

'What God can do for you'
Similar to the previous heading, there is sometimes a message preached in churches which implies that if you become a Christian then God will make you happy, wealthy and prosperous. Thus, some folk seek to become 'Christians' with the hope that they will receive material blessings from God. As discussed above, this is a dangerous message to preach in isolation, and can lead people astray. Of course God can and does make us happy when we are in a true and right relationship with Him. He also makes us prosperous, but not necessarily in the areas of wealth and material possessions. Those who have been blessed with wealth bear additional responsibilities and are exhorted to 'do good works, be generous and ready to share with others' (1 Tim. 6:18). However, for the Christian who has sought forgiveness for their sins by God's free grace and mercy, through the death and resurrection of the Lord Jesus, true prosperity lies in knowing that your sins are forgiven and that you have eternal life through the blood of the Lord Jesus, for 'God pardons those who humbly repent, and truly believe the gospel' (*Anglican Prayer Book*).

Holy Scripture warns us against false teaching and those who 'think that religion is a way to become rich'

(1 Tim. 6:5). The apostle Paul continues, 'Those who want to get rich fall into temptation and are caught in the trap of many foolish and harmful desires, which pull them down to ruin and destruction' (1 Tim. 6:9). Further, in the Old Testament we read in the book of Ecclesiastes, 'If you long to be rich you will never get all you want. It is useless' (Eccles. 5:10). True riches are to be found in Jesus Christ alone. Prayerfully read what the apostle Paul says about true riches in 1 Timothy 6.

Think also on the parable of the rich fool (Luke 12:13-21), who had so many crops that he decided to build himself newer, bigger barns in which to store all his crops (v.18). He considered himself lucky and decided to take life easy, eat, drink and enjoy himself (v.19). 'But God said to him "You fool"' (v.20) and that very night the man died. Let this be a sober warning to us about spending all our time accumulating material wealth and possessions, instead of spending our time doing things which bring glory to God. Let us seek to store up 'riches in heaven, where they will never decrease, because no thief can get to them, and no moth can destroy them' (Luke12:33).

In closing this section then, and referring back to the heading 'What God can do for you', my preference is to take a speech of the American President, John F. Kennedy, and adapt it slightly. Kennedy once famously said to the American people, 'Think not what your country can do for you, but what you can do for your country'. In the same vein I think it would be a good thing if all Christians adopted the saying, 'Think not what God can do for you, but what you can do for God'. Do not try to become a Christian just because you think God will give you great wealth and prosperity.

This path will always end in failure. Come humbly before God, acknowledging your sins and asking for His forgiveness. Then seek His will for you so that you can glorify Him through the way in which you live your life, in accordance with His holy Word.

Tithing

Tithing is an area which a lot of Christians struggle with. Most Christians understand that a figure of 10 per cent is in the debate somewhere, but are unclear as to whether this relates to pre-tax income or post-tax income. Also, is the 10 per cent figure to be seen as a minimum or maximum number when it comes to tithing? Finally, an often-asked question is whether paying income tax performs part of the role of tithing?

Tithing, as found in Holy Scripture, is the custom of giving a tenth of one's property for religious purposes. We see an example of the custom in Genesis 28:22 when Jacob makes a vow to God saying, 'I will give you a tenth of everything I have' as a sign of thanksgiving and worship to Him. We see an even earlier example in Genesis 14:20 when Abraham gave the priest Melchizedek a tenth of all the loot he had recovered from a battle, as a thanksgiving and praise to be offered up to God.

Further evidence of tithing can be found in Leviticus, the Old Testament book which contains regulations for worship and religious ceremonies in ancient Israel. The book sets out the ways in which God's people are to worship Him and to live their lives so as to maintain their relationship with Him. We find in Leviticus 27:30 'One-tenth of all the produce of the land, whether grain or fruit, belongs to the Lord'. And again in verse 32, 'One out of every ten animals belongs to the Lord'.

This message is taken up again in Proverbs 3:9 where we find the words 'Honour the Lord by making Him an offering from the best of all that your land produces'.

Later on in the Old Testament we find disturbing words in the book of the prophet Malachi, whose concern was that priests and people alike were drifting away from God. They were not living as God intended them to, in accordance with His teaching, and they were cheating God by not giving Him the offerings which were rightly due to him. In particular we read that God said: 'I ask you, is it right for a person to cheat God? Of course not, yet you are cheating me. 'How?' you ask. In the matter of tithes and offerings' (Mal. 3:8).

There can be a temptation to dismiss what the Old Testament says, arguing that Jesus came to change all that, and that the New Testament is the part of the Bible we should concentrate on. Beware, this is folly indeed. Jesus Himself many times referred to the Old Testament – what it says about Him, and about the godly lives lived by many Old Testament characters such as Abraham, Moses and David, to name just a few. Indeed, in the book of Leviticus we find the words that Jesus calls the second great commandment, 'Love your neighbour as you love yourself' (Lev. 19:18). Therefore, it would be wrong of us to dismiss what the Old Testament says about matters such as tithing.

If we dwell on these passages and pray about the issue, then I think it is clear that as Christians we are encouraged to give to God at least 10 percent of our income, to be used to His glory and praise and in the furtherance of His Kingdom. If we choose to give more than 10 percent then I think we should feel free to do so, out of our love for Him and what He has done for us by saving us from our sins, through the death and resurrection of His only Son, Jesus Christ.

Another important issue to consider as part of our overall tithing, or giving, is the support and upkeep of the church which we attend. It is sometimes easy to forget that the church we attend has to be maintained, so that it remains structurally sound. This may involve ongoing work to the fabric of the building such as the roof, walls or windows. It also has running costs which need to be covered, such as lighting, heating, cleaning and maintenance of the grounds around the building. In addition, our church may also have outreach commitments, missionary support commitments and other ministry activities which require some sort of financial outlay. As Christians it is important for us to take a shared responsibility in the costs of maintaining and running the church which we attend. The Bible points us to this responsibility in passages such as Exodus 30:11-16, where the people were encouraged to provide funds for the upkeep of the tent of the Lord's presence. Also, in Nehemiah 10:32 we read that the people undertook that 'Every year we will each contribute five grammes of silver to help pay the expenses of the Temple'.

Therefore it is vital that we attend church annual meetings, when the financial accounts of the church are presented, so that we fully understand the costs involved in maintaining and running the church. Alternatively, ask to see a copy of the latest annual accounts. Armed with that information, try to roughly work out how much each member of the church would need to give each year (or week) to meet the total costs. It is a reasonably easy sum to work out – find out from your minister or church wardens how many current members there are attending the church, then divide the total costs by the number of members and you will roughly have the annual amount required per member to meet all of the costs. I would then encourage you to compare this amount prayerfully with the amount you are currently giving. I fully understand that some people will simply not have the financial resources to meet whatever the figure is, so perhaps there is a need for those who have more to consider giving more. Remember that 'Much is required from the person to whom much is given; much more is required from the person to whom much more is given' (Luke12:48). We should all prayerfully seek God's guidance for us personally in this matter and allow ourselves to be guided by His Holy Spirit.

Whatever amount we decide to give, let us pray that we do so with a happy heart and with no sense of reluctance, for 'God loves the one who gives gladly' (2 Cor. 9:7).

The question of whether our tithing should be based on pre-tax income or post-tax income is an interesting one, which requires further discussion. Let us be clear first of all that God understands that we have to pay taxes, which are used to support the very fabric of the society in which we live. In three of the four gospels we find instruction in the words of Jesus, when the Pharisees were trying to trick Him into saying that people shouldn't pay money to Rome, which was anti-Christian in its views and actions. He said, 'Pay the Emperor what belongs to the Emperor and pay God what belongs to God' (Matt. 22.21; Mark 12.17; Luke 20.25). Additionally, Paul says, 'Everyone must obey the state authorities, because no authority exists without God's permission' (Rom. 13:1). Both of these passages are making it clear that we should pay our taxes because in doing so we are demonstrating that we are law-abiding citizens and thus bringing glory to God.

Ultimately the question of using a pre-tax or post-tax basis for our tithing is a personal one, and one which I would encourage you to pray about. But don't get too hung up on the issue. The Bible tells us of the poor widow's offering and Jesus' response to what He saw. In Luke 21:1 we find that 'Jesus looked around and saw rich men dropping their gifts in the temple treasury, and He also saw a very poor widow dropping in two little copper coins'. Now, let us ask ourselves who put most into the temple treasury. It is likely that the rich men put the largest amount in monetary terms, certainly well in excess of the two copper coins the poor widow placed in the treasury. However, Jesus observes, 'I tell you that this poor widow put in more than all the others. For the others offered their gifts from what they had to spare of their riches, but she, poor as she is, gave all she had to live on' (Luke 21:3-4). Let us learn from Jesus' words and beware of measuring our offerings in human terms; that is, how much in monetary value we give. Instead let us strive to be like the poor widow who gave freely of the little she had, because of her love for God. God does not want us to be begrudging givers. Instead He wants us to be happy givers, who do so because we love Him. 'Each one should give then as he has decided, not with regret or out of a sense of duty' (2 Cor. 9:7).

In viewing the question of whether paying income tax performs part of the role of tithing we need look no further than the Bible passages quoted earlier in this section, such as Genesis 28:22 and Leviticus 27:30. Both of these passages make it clear that tithing is the act of giving **to God** a tenth of all that he has blessed us with, not a tenth to be split between giving to God and paying our taxes, which are our contribution towards the support of society generally.

Lastly, no matter how much you give, do it quietly and without fuss. Jesus said, 'Do not make a big show of it, as the hypocrites do in the houses of worship and on the streets. They do it so that people will praise them. I assure you, they have already been paid in full'. Instead He exhorts us to 'do it in such a way that even your closest friend will not know about it. Then it will be a private matter and your Father, who sees what you do in private, will reward you' (Matt. 6:2-4).

Missionary support

I would take this opportunity to encourage you to become involved in supporting missionary work of some description, if you are not already doing so. The giving of something out of all that we have is encouraged in the Bible ('Give to others and God will give to you', Luke 6:38) and I would be failing in my duty when talking about personal finances if I did not encourage you to also plan to set aside something out of what you have to support missionary work of some kind.

There is good biblical evidence of instruction to Christians to support fellow believers. The apostle Paul exhorts us in his first letter to the church in Corinth to 'put aside some money, in proportion to what you have earned' (1 Cor. 16:2) for the help and support of missionary work, and this is something we should give prayerful thought and consideration. For, as Paul goes on in his second letter to the Corinthians, 'Remember that the person who sows few seeds will have a small crop; the one who sows many seeds will have a large crop' (2 Cor. 9:6). He is referring here to the blessings we receive from giving to help others. The more we give, the more we are blessed – not necessarily in financial terms, but in other ways. However, it is important to remember that we should give freely and not in the expectation that in doing so we will receive blessings. We should do it out of love for others and to please our heavenly Father. Paul says, 'Each one should give, then, as he has decided, not with regret or out of a sense of duty; for God loves the one who gives gladly' (2 Cor. 9:7).

I do not want to mislead people here, so let me be clear that it is important to remember that giving a little of what we have will not earn us our way into heaven, as some people are mistakenly informed. Please do not give to others just because you think that in doing so you will be saved, 'for it is by God's grace that you have been saved through faith. It is not the result of your own efforts, but God's gift' (Eph. 2:8-9). Remember at all times that we are saved by God's grace alone, through faith, not by our good deeds or actions. However, as saved Christians, giving towards missionary work is one way in which we may please our heavenly Father and show our love for Him, by supporting His workers in the mission field, where 'the harvest is large but there are few workers to gather it in' (Matt. 9:37).

If you are unsure about which mission to support, then pray about it and ask God to show you a mission in which you can become involved by offering your support, either financial or in other ways such as your time, or using the skills which God has blessed you with. Also, speak to your church minister, who will probably be able to supply you with information on a number of mission agencies, so that you can investigate those agencies further and pray about which one to support.

Make a Will

Whilst not directly linked to money, the making of a Will is an important part of the overall subject of personal finance, so it is appropriate that I include some brief information on the subject.

A Will is a legal document which sets out how you would like your money and possessions, collectively called your 'estate', distributed in the event of your death.

It is important to make a Will because, simply put, if you do not then your estate may be distributed in a way which you would not want it to be. Let us look at a simple example to illustrate the point.

Assume that you are married and that you have two children. Now you may want to leave some particular possession or part of your estate to your children rather than your spouse. If you do not make a Will then, generally, under law the entirety of your estate will pass to your spouse, assuming he or she survives you. Therefore, your estate would not be distributed as you intended.

This is a simple example but it illustrates the point that by making a Will you remove any uncertainty about how you want your estate to be distributed. This can help prevent family feuds and unhappy arguments after your death, so it is better to have it all set out in writing beforehand.

Another reason for making a Will may be taxation issues, where having your estate distributed in accordance with Common Law, rather than in the way you intended, may result in unnecessary taxes being due.

Drawing up a Will is a complex task and the advice of a professional should be sought when doing this. A solicitor will normally be the first person you talk to about this, and they will advise you on the best way to go about drawing up your Will, bearing in mind all of the legal and taxation issues which may be involved.

Financial Education for Children

Children learn many things at school. They learn reading, writing, mathematics, history, physical education and so on. One thing they are not taught, however, is how to manage money. This is where parents have a vital role to play in the education of their children.

The Bible tells us that parents should educate their children. We find in the Old Testament book of Proverbs, 'Teach a child how he should live, and he will remember it all his life' (Prov. 22:6). In the New Testament we find the words: 'Bring them (children) up with Christian discipline and instruction' (Eph. 6:4). It is certain that our Lord Himself learnt the skills of carpentry from His earthly father, Joseph, who was a carpenter by trade. Jesus would have been exposed to the daily work of the carpenter and certainly would have picked up some of the skills of that trade. Therefore, there is a precedent set for parents to pass on the experience and knowledge they have gained to their children.

I would strongly urge parents to provide their children with a basic understanding of the value of money and how to handle it responsibly. In fact, I would go so far as to say that parents have a moral obligation to do this. Believe me, in doing so you will be teaching them one of the most important life skills, and one which they will have reason to thank you for as they get older and have to start to manage their own financial affairs. By teaching them how to manage their finances responsibly you will be shielding them from what may potentially be an area which will cause them much heartache and difficulty in the future – something I am sure all parents would want to do for their children.

A simple and effective way of teaching children the value of money and how to handle it is to give them an allowance, or pocket money, instead of just buying everything for them. Set out the ground rules with your children from the outset, agreeing the amount and frequency of the allowance, what items the children will need to buy for themselves using their allowance, and what items you will buy for them. This is important if you are to avoid misunderstandings in the future. For example, if you tell your child at the outset that they have to use their own money or allowance to buy sweets, then if they ask you to buy them some sweets in a shop you can remind them of the original agreement, so there is no doubt about what is and isn't to be bought by you.

Provide loving guidance to your child by helping them understand that once they have spent all their money, that is it until their next allowance is due. For example, if they are in a sweet shop and are about to use all their allowance on some purchases, remind them that if they do that then they will not have any money left over to buy more sweets until their next allowance is due. This will help them to plan ahead, or budget, so that they keep enough money back to see them through until their next allowance is due. You can see the similarity here in adult life where we need to plan ahead, or budget, from one pay period to the next.

It is important to be firm and resolute in your guidance to your child, and do not give in to demands for things to be bought which the child should be buying with their own money or allowance. Some parents these days seem to think that saying 'No' to their child is wrong and that if they do so their child will, in some way, not love them anymore. This is complete rubbish. Children need and want you to set boundaries for them, so that they understand what is acceptable and what is not acceptable. By providing guidance and ground rules for your child in the area of money, you will be demonstrating love of the highest order – love which will serve your child well in the future in assisting them to manage their finances and help prevent them getting into all sorts of financial difficulties. If you do give in to the demands of your child, you will not be doing them any favours whatsoever because, when they are older, no-one will be there to buy them things they want when they don't have any money left. If they are taught at an early age how to use their money wisely, they are much more likely to be responsible with their finances when they are older.

Appendix – Example of Personal Budget

	Monthly	Quarterly	Annually
Income (net of tax)	**£2,300**		**£27,600**
Expenditure:			
Rent/Morgage	£500		£6,000
Gas	£20	£60	£240
Electric	£30	£90	£360
Telephone/Internet	£30	£90	£360
Mobile Telephone	£20		£240
Food	£400		£4,800
General Expenses (clothes, spending money, etc)	£200		£2,400
Insurances (Life and Home)	£100		£1,200
Credit Cards	£50		£600
Personal Loans	£100		£1,200
Vehicle costs (petrol, tax, servicing, insurance)	£200		£2,400
Holidays	£50		£600
Water Rates	£35	£105	£420
Council Rates	£83		£996
Tithe	£250		£3,000
Mission Giving	£50		£600
Contingency	£50		£600
Total Expenditure	**£2,168**		**£26,016**
Surplus (Income - Expenditure)	**£132**		**£1,584**

THE UNHEEDED CHRIST

JESUS DEMANDS SERIOUS OBEDIENCE

DAVID COOK

The Unheeded Christ
Jesus Demands Serious Obedience
David Cook

Jesus Christ is a provocative, uncompromising teacher. Yet it is easy to become so accustomed to Jesus' words that they become old friends – comfortable, familiar, unchallenging. We get so used to Him that we forget to take notice of what He commands us to do.

Jesus demands serious obedience from His people in all areas of life. Here He challenges us about crucial issues – loving enemies, forgiveness, sex, ambition, adultery, wealth accumulation, revenge, impending judgement, resolving tension between Christians, and self-delusion.

His words come across as fresh, immediate, wise, authentic and discerning. Listen to Him again – and this time, don't let Him go unheeded.

David is the Principal and Director of the School of Preaching at Sydney Missionary and Bible College (SMBC). He is a Presbyterian minister and a graduate of SMBC and Moore Theological College. Prior to formal studies and pastoral ministry, David worked in the Economic Research Department of the Reserve Bank. He has spoken at a number of Christian Conventions including Keswick. David is married to Maxine, and they have five adult children and eight grandchildren.

ISBN 978-1-84550-369-7

Christian Focus Publications
publishes books for all ages

Our mission statement –

STAYING FAITHFUL
In dependence upon God we seek to help make His infallible Word, the Bible, relevant. Our aim is to ensure that the Lord Jesus Christ is presented as the only hope to obtain forgiveness of sin, live a useful life and look forward to heaven with Him.

REACHING OUT
Christ's last command requires us to reach out to our world with His gospel. We seek to help fulfil that by publishing books that point people towards Jesus and help them develop a Christ-like maturity. We aim to equip all levels of readers for life, work, ministry and mission.

Books in our adult range are published in three imprints.

Christian Focus contains popular works including biographies, commentaries, basic doctrine and Christian living. Our children's books are also published in this imprint.

Mentor focuses on books written at a level suitable for Bible College and seminary students, pastors, and other serious readers. The imprint includes commentaries, doctrinal studies, examination of current issues and church history.

Christian Heritage contains classic writings from the past.

Christian Focus Publications, Ltd
Geanies House, Fearn,
Ross-shire, IV20 1TW, Scotland, United Kingdom
info@christianfocus.com

Our titles are available from
www.christianfocus.com